Healthy Plates

PROTEINS

VALERIE BODDEN

Published by Creative Education and Creative Paperbacks | P.O. Box 227, Mankato, Minnesota 56002
Creative Education and Creative Paperbacks are imprints of The Creative Company
www.thecreativecompany.us

Design by Liddy Walseth | Production by Christine Vanderbeek
Printed in the United States of America

Photographs by Alamy (Art of Food, D. Hurst), Corbis (Peter Reali), Dreamstime (Yen Hung Lin, Andrzej Tokarski), iStockphoto (gojak, NormaZaro), Shutterstock (Andrey_Kuzmin, Paul Cowan, Lesya Dolyuk, Fotoluminate LLC, hin255, Pavel Hlystov, Hurst Photo, indigolotos, KonstantinGushcha, konzeptm, Olga Miltsova, Elena M. Tarasova, Timmary, Tsekhmister), SuperStock (Blend Images)

Library of Congress Cataloging-in-Publication Data
Bodden, Valerie. | Proteins / Valerie Bodden. | p. cm. — (Healthy plates) | Summary: An early reader's introduction to the connections between the proteins food group and staying healthy, benefits of proteins such as meat, nutritional concepts such as vitamins, and recipe instructions. Includes bibliographical references and index. | ISBN 978-1-60818-511-5 (hardcover) ISBN 978-1-62832-111-1 (pbk) | 1. Proteins in human nutrition—Juvenile literature. I. Title.
TX553.P7B66 2015 | 613.2'82—dc23 | 2014000711

CCSS: RI.1.1, 2, 4, 5, 6, 7; RI.2.2, 5, 6, 7, 10; RI.3.1, 5, 7, 8; RF.1.1, 3, 4; RF.2.3, 4

First Edition 9 8 7 6 5 4 3 2 1

TABLE OF CONTENTS

Growing Up

Your body needs food to give it energy and help it grow. But not all foods are good for you. Healthy foods contain the **nutrients** (*NOO-tree-unts*) your body needs to be at its best. Healthy foods are put into five food groups: dairy, fruits, **grains**, proteins, and vegetables. Your body needs foods from each food group every day.

HEALTHY FOODS CAN TASTE GOOD AND ARE GOOD FOR YOU, TOO.

Protein Group

Foods in the protein group have the nutrient protein. Protein helps your body grow. There are proteins in your bones, muscles, **organs**, teeth, hair, and skin.

PROTEINS ARE LIKE THE TINY BUILDING BLOCKS OF THE BODY.

Meats such as beef and pork are part of the protein group. So are chicken, turkey, and seafood. Eggs, nuts, beans, and seeds are also proteins.

SALMON IS A HEALTHY SEAFOOD. A PIECE OF SALMON IS RICH IN PROTEIN.

Vitamins and Nutrients

Foods in the protein group have many **vitamins**. Eggs have Vitamin A. Vitamin A helps your eyesight. Nuts and seeds have Vitamin E to help form blood **cells** and muscles.

YOU CAN SCRAMBLE EGGS AND MIX IN VEGETABLES TO MAKE AN OMELET.

Many foods in the protein group have B vitamins. B vitamins keep your brain and heart healthy. They help your body turn food into energy and form blood cells.

A DIP CALLED HUMMUS IS MADE FROM CHICKPEAS AND HAS PROTEIN.

Meats, eggs, and beans also have iron. Iron helps your blood take **oxygen** to your body's cells. Seafood has nutrients called omega-3 fatty acids. These can keep your **blood pressure** low so that your heart does not have to work too hard.

CHILI IS A GOOD WAY TO PACK IN PROTEINS LIKE MEAT AND BEANS.

How Much?

Most kids should eat about two to five ounces (56.7–142 g) of proteins every day. One hamburger counts as about two ounces (56.7 g). One egg or one tablespoon (15 ml) of peanut butter is about one ounce (28.3 g). People who are older or more active can eat more protein-rich foods.

Healthy Living

It is easy to get enough protein.
Have a turkey sandwich for lunch.
Try some fish for supper. Dip
apple slices in peanut butter
for a snack.

Eating protein-rich foods is part of being healthy. Exercising is another part. Try to move your body an hour every day. Exercising and eating healthy can be fun— and can make you feel good, too!

IF YOU LIVE NEAR WATER, YOU CAN SURF AND SWIM AS EXERCISE!

MAKE A PROTEIN SNACK:

PEANUT BUTTER-BANANA POPS

1 BANANA

2 TBSP. PEANUT BUTTER

1 HANDFUL CHOPPED PEANUTS

Peel the banana, and break it in half. Put a Popsicle stick into the wider end of each half. Spread each banana with a thin layer of peanut butter. Then roll it in chopped nuts. Put the bananas on a plate in the freezer until the peanut butter hardens. Enjoy your protein-packed snack!

GLOSSARY

blood pressure—how hard a person's blood pushes against the blood vessels, or tubes that carry blood through the body

cells—tiny parts that make up all living things

grains—parts of some kinds of grasses, such as wheat or oats, that are used to make bread and other foods

nutrients—the parts of food that your body uses to make energy, grow, and stay healthy

organs—parts of the body that do a certain job; the heart and eyes are organs

oxygen—a gas, or type of air, that people need to breathe

vitamins—nutrients found in foods that are needed to keep your body healthy and working well

READ MORE

Head, Honor. *Healthy Eating*. Mankato, Minn.: Sea-to-Sea, 2013.

Kalz, Jill. *Meats and Protein*. North Mankato, Minn.: Smart Apple Media, 2004.

Llewellyn, Claire. *Healthy Eating*. Laguna Hills, Calif.: QEB, 2006.

WEBSITES

My Plate Kids' Place
http://www.choosemyplate.gov/kids/index.html
Check out games, activities, and recipes about eating healthy.

PBS Kids: Healthy Eating Games
http://pbskids.org/games/healthyeating.html
Play games that help you learn about healthy foods.

Note: Every effort has been made to ensure that the websites listed above are suitable for children, that they have educational value, and that they contain no inappropriate material. However, because of the nature of the Internet, it is impossible to guarantee that these sites will remain active indefinitely or that their contents will not be altered.

INDEX